Health

Karen Durrie

MEDIA ENHANCED BOOKS
AV²
BY WEIGL™
ADDED VALUE • AUDIO VISUAL

AV² provides enriched content that supplements and complements this book. Weigl's AV² books strive to create inspired learning and engage young minds in a total learning experience.

Your AV² Media Enhanced books come alive with...

Go to **www.av2books.com**, and enter this book's unique code.

BOOK CODE

L490441

AV² by Weigl brings you media enhanced books that support active learning.

Audio
Listen to sections of the book read aloud.

Video
Watch informative video clips.

Embedded Weblinks
Gain additional information for research.

Try This!
Complete activities and hands-on experiments.

Key Words
Study vocabulary, and complete a matching word activity.

Quizzes
Test your knowledge.

Slide Show
View images and captions, and prepare a presentation.

... and much, much more!

Published by AV² by Weigl
350 5th Avenue, 59th Floor New York, NY 10118
Website: www.av2books.com   www.weigl.com

Library of Congress Cataloging-in-Publicataion Data available upon request.
Fax 1-866-44-WEIGL for the attention of the Publishing Records department.

ISBN 978-1-61690-950-5 (hard cover)

Printed in the United States of America in North Mankato, Minnesota
1 2 3 4 5 6 7 8 9 0 15 14 13 12 11

062011
WEP030611

Project Coordinator: Karen Durrie Art Director: Terry Paulhus

Weigl acknowledges Getty Images as the primary image supplier for this title.

Health

CONTENTS

Some community workers help us to be healthy.

4

Doctor

Nurse

Optometrist

Fitness Teacher

Nutritionist

Counselor

Dentist

I make sure your body is healthy.
I help when you are sick or hurt.

6

I am a doctor.

I show you how
to keep your body
strong and healthy.

I am a fitness teacher.

I check your health.
I weigh and measure you.
I may give you a shot.

I am a nurse.

11

I look at your eyes and test how well you can see.

I am an optometrist.

I teach you about
the best foods to eat.

I am a nutritionist.

I check your teeth and gums
to make sure they are healthy.

I am a dentist.

I talk with you about your thoughts and feelings.

I am a counselor.

When people are healthy, communities are healthy.

How do you stay healthy?

HEALTH FACTS

People with common interests can form a community. Each job in health plays a different role in keeping people healthy. The health community also helps people meet lifestyle goals, such as being fit and eating well. Read below to learn more about these helpers.

Pages 4-5

We do many things to keep healthy. We exercise and eat good food. We also visit health professionals so we can maintain our good health. Health workers tell us how to look after ourselves. They also take care of us if we have health problems.

Pages 6–7

We go to doctors for checkups when we are not sick. At a checkup, a doctor measures how healthy we are. The doctor may listen to our heart and lungs and look in our ears, eyes, nose, and throat.

Pages 8–9

Fitness teachers work at many places in our communities. Some of them teach in schools. Others may work outdoors, or at swimming pools and gyms, teaching special classes like yoga.

Pages 10–11

When we go to the doctor, it is often the nurse we talk to first. The nurse may check our blood pressure and take our temperature. Nurses also work in hospitals, taking care of patients, and in schools, talking to students about health and looking after them if they do not feel well.

WORD LIST

Research has shown that as much as 65 percent of all written material published in English is made up of 300 words. These 300 words cannot be taught using pictures or learned by sounding them out. They must be recognized by sight. This book contains 38 common sight words to help young readers improve their reading fluency and comprehension. This book also teaches young readers several important content words, such as proper nouns. These words are paired with pictures to aid in learning and improve understanding.

Page	Sight Words First Appearance
4	be, help, in, our, some, to
6	are, I, is, make, or, when, you, your
7	a
8	and, how, keep, show
10	give, may
12	at, can, eyes, look, see, well
13	an
14	about, eat, foods, the
16	they
18	talk, thoughts, with
20	people
21	do

Page	Content Words First Appearance
4	community, workers
5	counselor, dentist, doctor, nurse, nutritionist, optometrist, teacher
6	body
10	health, shot
16	gums, teeth
18	feelings